A
MOTHER'S
TOUCH

A Tribute to the Influence and Love of Mothers

Cover image: *Le Matin Dans Le Jardin* © Heidi Presse. Licensed by The Greenwich Workshop, Inc.
For print information please visit www.greenwichworkshop.com.

Cover and book design by Christina Ashby, © 2007 by Covenant Communications, Inc.

Published by Covenant Communications, Inc.,
American Fork, Utah

Printed in China
First Printing: March 2008

14 13 12 11 10 09 08   10 9 8 7 6 5 4 3 2 1

ISBN 13: 978-1-59811-556-7
ISBN 10: 1-59811-556-1

A
MOTHER'S
TOUCH

$\mathscr{I}$ looked on child-rearing not only as a work of love and duty but as a profession that was fully as interesting and challenging as any honorable profession in the world and one that demanded the best that I could bring it.

—*Rose Kennedy*

5

$\mathcal{E}$verybody knows that a good mother gives her children a feeling of trust and stability. She is their earth. She is the one they can count on for the things that matter most of all. She is their food and their bed and the extra blanket when it grows cold in the night; she is their warmth and their health and their shelter; she is the one they want to be near when they cry. She is the only person in the whole world in a whole lifetime who can be these things to her children. There is no substitute for her.

—Katharine Butler Hathaway

*L*ittle girls,
like butterflies,
need no
excuse.

—*Robert A.
Heinlein*

A mother laughs our laughter,
Sheds our tears,
Returns our love,
Fears our fears.
She lives our joys,
Cares our cares,
And all our hopes and
dreams she shares.

—*Julia Summers*

$\mathcal{M}$otherhood brings as much joy as ever, but it still brings boredom, exhaustion, and sorrow too. Nothing else ever will make you as happy or as sad, as proud or as tired, for nothing is quite as hard as helping a person develop his own individuality especially while you struggle to keep your own.

—*Marguerite Kelly and Elia Parsons*

13

*I*n seed
time, learn; in
harvest, teach;
in winter, enjoy.

—*William Blake*

You never realize how much your mother loves you till you explore the attic—and find every letter you ever sent her, every finger painting, clay pot, bead necklace, Easter chicken, cardboard Santa Claus, paperlace Mother's Day card and school report since day one.

—*Pam Brown*

The mother, more than any other, affects the moral and spiritual part of the children's character. She is their constant companion and teacher in formative years. The child is ever imitating and assimilating the mother's nature. It is only in after life that men gaze backward and behold how a mother's hand and heart of love molded their young lives and shaped their destiny.

— *E.W. Caswell*

*H*eaven
is at the feet of
mothers.

—*Roebuck*

21

When God thought of mother, He must have laughed with satisfaction and framed it quickly—so rich, so deep, so divine, so full of soul, power, and beauty was the conception.

—*Henry Ward Beecher*

$\mathcal{C}$ultivating
friendships
provides
nourishment
for your heart.

—*Anonymous*

A house is no home
unless it contains food and fire
for the mind as well as for the body.

—*Margaret Fuller*

$\mathcal{A}$ mother's love is like the sun
rising in the sky each day —
a constant source of warmth
and comfort.

—*Anonymous*

29

*I*n all my efforts to learn to read, my mother shared fully my ambition and sympathized with me and aided me in every way she could. If I have done anything in life worth attention, I feel sure that I inherited the disposition from my mother.

—*Booker T. Washington*

The best academy, a mother's knee.

—*James R. Lowell*

$\mathcal{I}$t is a
wonderful
seasoning of all
enjoyments to
think of those
we love.

—*Jean Baptiste
Moliere*

*N*o language can express
the power and beauty and heroism
of a mother's love.

—*Edwin Hubble Chapin*

$\mathcal{B}$iology

is the least of

what makes

someone a

mother.

—*Oprah Winfrey*

$\mathscr{I}$ shall never forget my mother, for it was she who planted and nurtured the first seeds of good within me.

—*Immanuel Kant*

*H*ope
is the thing
with feathers
that perches
in the soul
and sings the
tune without
the words and
never stops
at all.

— *Emily Dickinson*

$\mathcal{T}$he goodness of home is not dependent on wealth, or spaciousness, or beauty, or luxury. Everything depends on the mother.

—*G. W. E. Russell*

There is a garden in every childhood, an enchanted place where colors are brighter, the air softer, and the morning more fragrant than ever again.

—*Elizabeth Lawrence*

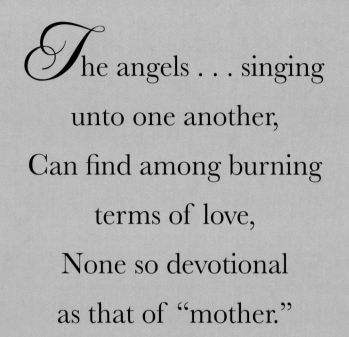

$\mathcal{T}$he angels . . . singing
unto one another,
Can find among burning
terms of love,
None so devotional
as that of "mother."

—*Edgar Allen Poe*

She is my first, great love. She was a wonderful, rare woman—you do not know; as strong, and steadfast, and generous as the sun. She could be as swift as a white whiplash, and as kind and gentle as warm rain, and as steadfast as the irreducible earth beneath us.

—*D H Lawrence*

51

$\mathcal{A}$ mother
is she who can
take the place
of all others
but whose
place no one
else can take.

—*Cardinal Mermillod*

The future destiny of the child is always the work of the mother.

— *Napoleon Bonaparte*

There never was a woman like her. She was gentle as a dove and brave as a lioness . . . The memory of my mother and her teachings were, after all, the only capital I had to start life with, and on that capital I have made my way.

—*Andrew Jackson*

$\mathcal{T}$he heart
that loves is
always young.

—*Greek proverb*

59

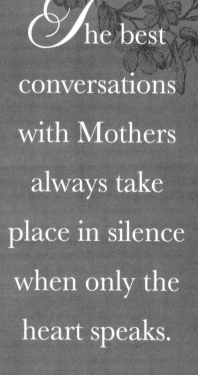

*T*he best conversations with Mothers always take place in silence when only the heart speaks.

— *Carrie Latet*

There was never a great man who had not a great mother.

—*Olive Schreiner*

The noblest calling in the world is motherhood. True motherhood is the most beautiful of all arts, the greatest of all professions. She who can paint a masterpiece, or who can write a book that will influence millions, deserves the plaudits and admiration of mankind; but she who rears successfully a family of healthy, beautiful sons and daughters whose immortal souls will exert an influence throughout the ages long after paintings shall have faded, and books and statues shall have decayed or been destroyed, deserves the highest honor that man can give, and the choicest blessings of God.

—*David O. McKay*

The mother loves her child most divinely, not when she surrounds him with comfort and anticipates his wants, but when she resolutely holds him to the highest standards and is content with nothing less than his best.

—*Hamilton Wright Mabie*

 **Mother**
is the heartbeat
in the home;
and without
her, there seems
to be no heart
throb.

—*Leroy Brownlow*

$\mathcal{A}$ mother is the truest friend we have when trials, heavy and sudden, fall upon us; when adversity takes the place of prosperity.

—*Washington Irving*

Children and
mothers never
truly part—
Bound in the
beating of each
other's heart.

—*Charlotte Gray*

$\mathcal{M}$other's
love grows
by giving.

—*Charles Lamb*

$\mathcal{S}$imple days bring simple joys.

— *Emily Lawless*

ll thy
children shall
be taught of
the Lord; and
great shall be
the peace of
thy children.

—*Isaiah 54:13*

It seems to me that my mother was the most splendid woman I ever knew. . . . I have met a lot of people knocking around the world since, but I have never met a more thoroughly refined woman than my mother. If I have amounted to anything, it will be due to her.

—*Charles Chaplin*

 **Mighty**
is the force of
motherhood!

—*George Eliot*

$\mathcal{H}$owever many years she lived she should never forget that first morning when her garden began to grow.

—*Frances Hodgson Burnett*, The Secret Garden

You never
get over being
a child, as long
as you have
a mother to
go to.

—*Sarah Orne
Jewett*

$\mathcal{C}$hildren are
the anchors
that hold a
mother to life.

—*Sophocles*

omen as
the guardians of
children possess a
great power. They
are the moulders
of their children's
personalities and
the arbiters of their
development.

—*Ann Oakley*

Who ran to help me when I fell,
And would some pretty story tell,
Or kiss the place to make it well?
My Mother.

—*Ann Taylor*

$\mathcal{I}$ cannot tell you how much I owe to the solemn word of my good mother.

—*Charles Haddon Spurgeon*